Quick Revision

KS3

History

Dave Martin

How to use this book

This book will help you learn and understand all the essential facts for Modern World History at Key Stage 3 level. It covers the twentieth century. Its A–Z approach means you can find the topic you need quickly and easily. Key words are highlighted in **bold** in the text.

Acknowledgements

Whilst every effort has been made to trace the copyright holders, in cases where this has been unsuccessful or if any have been inadvertently overlooked, the publisher will be pleased to make the necessary arrangements at the first opportunity.

Poetry excerpts on pages 42–43 © Siegfried Sassoon reproduced by kind permission of George Sassoon.

The publishers are grateful to Ford Motor Company Ltd for the image on page 16.

First published 2007
exclusively for WHSmith by
Hodder Murray, a member of the Hodder Headline group
338 Euston Road
London
NW1 3BH

Impression number   10 9 8 7 6 5 4 3 2 1
Year   2010 2009 2008 2007

Cover illustration by Sally Newton Illustrations.

Typeset by Starfish Design Editorial and Project Management Ltd

ISBN: 978 034 0 94309 0

Printed and bound in the UK by Hobbs the Printers Ltd.

Afghanistan

The country of Afghanistan was invaded by the **Soviet Union** in December 1979. The Soviet Union was trying to stop the Afghan Islamic guerrilla groups (the Mujahidin) from overthrowing the unpopular **Communist** government.

Many of the people of the southern Soviet Union were also followers of the Islamic religion and the Soviet government feared that they might be encouraged to rebel. The invasion was a disaster for Afghanistan. About 1 million Afghans died and millions fled abroad as refugees. It was also a disaster for the Soviet Union. The enormous cost crippled their economy, and the fighting showed up the poor quality of the Soviet army. In 1989, recognising that they could not win, the Soviet president Mikhail Gorbachev ordered a withdrawal. In the civil war that followed the Taliban came to power and imposed strict Muslim law on the population.

SEE ALSO Cold War

Appeasement

The policy of the governments of Britain and France towards **Adolf Hitler** (leader of Germany) and his aggressive foreign policy in the years leading up to the **Second World War** is known as appeasement. They believed that if they gave in to Hitler's demands then he would be satisfied. Many people in both countries did not want a repeat of the terrible loss of life of the **First World War** and so were very anxious to avoid another war. Some people, notably **Winston Churchill**, spoke out against this policy.

Armistice

An armistice is a truce or ceasefire. The ceasefire that ended fighting in the **First World War** came into effect at 11a.m. on 11 November 1918 – the eleventh hour of the eleventh day of the eleventh month of the fourth year of the war. We still commemorate this date each year. The poppies we wear are a reminder of the poppies that flowered amid the destruction of **trench warfare** on the **Western Front** in northern France and Belgium.

SEE ALSO **Korean War**

Assassination at Sarajevo

This was the assassination of Franz Ferdinand and his wife Sophie by Gavrilo Princip, a member of the Black Hand Gang, which took place in Sarajevo on 28 June 1914. As Franz Ferdinand was the heir to the throne of the Austro-Hungarian Empire and the Black Hand Gang were supported by Serbia, this provided an excuse for Austria to try to humiliate Serbia. This was the trigger that started the chain of events that led eventually to the outbreak of the **First World War**. Two deaths led to 8 million deaths.

SEE ALSO Triple Alliance and Triple Entente

Atomic bomb

During the **Second World War** both sides worked on developing new weapons. The most frightening was the atomic bomb which the Americans and British had ready by 1945. On 6 August 1945 a US bomber, the *Enola Gay*, dropped the first atomic bomb on the Japanese city of Hiroshima, killing 70,000 people. Three days later another atomic bomb was dropped on a second Japanese city, Nagasaki, killing 36,000 people. Japan surrendered and the Second World War was over.

The results of dropping the bomb were so horrific that as historians we have to ask why it was done.

Some possible reasons are:

- The Americans believed that the Japanese would never surrender, and that if they had to invade Japan hundreds of thousands of Americans would be killed.
- The bomb had cost a lot of money to develop and the Americans wanted to use it.
- The Americans wanted to show their military superiority to the **Soviet Union**.
- Some Americans believed that the Japanese deserved it because of their cruel treatment of prisoners of war.

When the US President Harry Truman heard of the bombing he said, 'This is the greatest thing in history'. It certainly marked the beginning of the nuclear age. During the **Cold War** that followed there was always the fear of a nuclear war and the possible extinction of the human race, especially after the Soviet Union tested its first atomic bomb in 1949.

SEE ALSO Oppenheimer, Robert

Attrition

The trenches on the **Western Front** in the **First World War** made defence stronger than attack and so a stalemate – or deadlock – developed. The generals on both sides adopted a policy of attrition – that is, to keep attacking to wear down the enemy so that their supply of men and equipment is used up first. If the enemy's casualties are higher than yours then the battle is a success for your side. This led to very high casualty figures. In some later twentieth-century wars increasing casualty figures made the war so unpopular that political leaders were forced to change their policies.

SEE ALSO Somme; Trench warfare; Verdun; Vietnam War; Ypres

Balance of power

At the start of the twentieth century there were fierce rivalries between the European countries. Their leaders tried to stop any one country from becoming too powerful and upsetting the balance of power. If no country felt strong enough to attack another then the peace would be kept. This was why they came together into alliances.

At the beginning of the twentieth century the strengths of the two sides were as follows:

Country	Soldiers	Warships	Submarines
Austria–Hungary	810,000	28	62
Germany	2,200,000	97	23
Italy	750,000	36	12
Britain	711,000	185	64
France	1,250,000	62	73
Russia	1,200,000	30	0

SEE ALSO Cold War; Triple Alliance and Triple Entente

Berlin Airlift/Blockade

Russian
American
British
French
Berlin Wall, 1961
Airport
Major Road
Railway

In June 1948 the Soviet leader, **Josef Stalin**, cut all road and rail links between West Berlin and the western half of Germany. This became known as the Berlin Blockade. He was trying to gain control of West Berlin and was unhappy at the Allies' plans to rebuild Germany. The Allies (Britain, France and the USA) flew supplies into the city to keep the people fed and warm – this was the Berlin Airlift. Realising his plan was failing, Stalin reopened road and rail links in May 1949.

How historians label this – Airlift or Blockade – can depend upon which side they think was at fault.

SEE ALSO Cold War; Communism; Iron Curtain

Berlin Wall, building of

In August 1961 the **Communist** East German government built a wall around the western half of the city of Berlin so that East Germans could no longer escape into the West by entering West Berlin. They were worried that so many skilled young people were leaving in search of better opportunities. Many East Germans were shot and killed trying to escape across the wall.

Berlin Wall, fall of

The wall became a hated symbol of **communism** to many Germans. On 9 November 1989, when the **Cold War** was coming to an end, the East German government ordered the gates in the wall to be opened and ordinary Berliners rushed to help tear the wall down.

SEE ALSO Reunification of Germany

Blitzkrieg

This is the German word for 'lightning war', the tactics used by Germany in the **Second World War**. This was a war based upon the fast movement of **tanks** and motorised troops supported by aircraft. It was entirely different from the static **trench warfare** of the **First World War** and helped to explain the great German successes in the early years of the war.

SEE ALSO Dunkirk

British Empire

The map on the next page shows all the countries in the British Empire in 1900. Most of these countries were called colonies and were ruled from Britain. (Canada was a dominion.) Some were countries where so many British people had settled that they had become British, some had been 'won' in wars and some had been claimed by British explorers.
It was proudly described as 'the Empire on which the Sun never set'.

SEE ALSO Colonialism; Imperialism

Continued overleaf

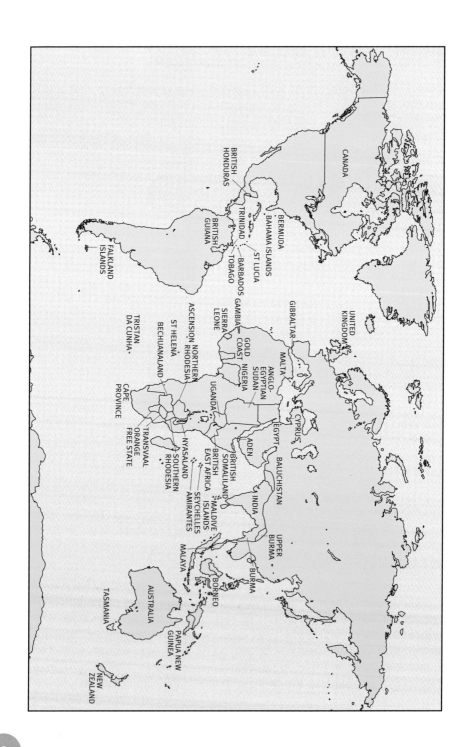

CANADA

BRITISH
HONDURAS

BERMUDA
BAHAMA ISLANDS

BRITISH
GUIANA

TRINIDAD

ST LUCIA
BARBADOS
TOBAGO

FALKLAND
ISLANDS

GIBRALTAR

UNITED
KINGDOM

GAMBIA
SIERRA
LEONE

GOLD
COAST

NIGERIA

MALTA

ANGLO-
EGYPTIAN
SUDAN

CYPRUS

EGYPT

BALUCHISTAN

UPPER
BURMA

ASCENSION

NORTHERN
RHODESIA

ST HELENA

TRISTAN
DA CUNHA

BECHUANALAND

UGANDA

CAPE
PROVINCE

TRANSVAAL

ORANGE
FREE STATE

NYASALAND

SOUTHERN
RHODESIA

BRITISH
SOMALILAND

BRITISH
EAST AFRICA

ADEN

AMIRANTES

MALDIVE
ISLANDS

SEYCHELLES

INDIA

BURMA

MALAYA

BORNEO

TASMANIA

AUSTRALIA

PAPUA NEW
GUINEA

NEW
ZEALAND

Capitalism

Capitalism is the system under which businesses are privately owned and run for the profit their owners can earn.

SEE ALSO Communism

Cause

A cause is a reason why something happens. As you know by now, nothing in history is simple so all events have more than one cause. They can sometimes be organised into types: trigger, short- or long-term, religious, social, economic, political.

So, for example, the system of alliances could be described as a long-term cause of the **First World War**, while the assassination of Franz Ferdinand could be described as a trigger cause.

SEE ALSO Consequence

Change

In history, change describes the idea that things do not stay the same.

SEE ALSO Continuity

Churchill, Winston

The politician Winston Churchill was one of the greatest opponents of **appeasement** before the **Second World War**. Once the war started it was obvious that this policy had failed and that Britain needed a new leader. In 1940 it was Churchill who became that leader and as prime minister he successfully led Britain throughout the war.

SEE ALSO Gallipoli; Iron Curtain

Cold War

After defeating Germany in the **Second World War** in 1945, the Allies fell out. The tension between the **Soviet Union** on one side and the USA and Britain on the other affected world affairs. These tensions never actually ended in open (or 'hot') war between the two sides, but they did get involved in other people's wars around the world. So this period is known as the Cold War.

The two sides competed in a number of ways, including:

- giving military support to opposing sides in the many localised wars, for example, Afghanistan, Vietnam
- using propaganda
- giving economic aid to their friends
- imposing trade sanctions on the other side's friends
- arms building, particularly nuclear weapons
- espionage or spying
- space exploration.

The Cold War ended in 1991 with the end of **communism** in the Soviet Union.

SEE ALSO Berlin Airlift/Blockade; Capitalism; Communism; Cuban Missile Crisis; Korean War; Olympic boycott

Colonialism

This is the taking over of smaller and generally weaker countries by more powerful countries to form colonies. The **British Empire** at the start of the twentieth century was one of the most extensive empires with a large number of colonies. An example further back in time would be the Roman Empire.

SEE ALSO Imperialism

Common Market

The name by which the European Economic Community was known in Britain after it was founded in 1958 under the Treaty of Rome. The original members were Belgium, Germany, France, Italy, Luxembourg and the Netherlands. Britain joined in 1973.

SEE ALSO European Union

Communism

Communism is the system in which all the businesses and industries are run and owned by the state on behalf of the people. It is based upon the ideas of **Karl Marx**. This is the system under which the **Soviet Union** was run.

SEE ALSO Capitalism

Consequence

A consequence is one effect of something happening. As you already know, nothing in history is simple, so any one event can have many consequences. An example might be the policy of *Glasnost* (openness) begun by Soviet president Mikhail Gorbachev. This ended in the fall of **communism** not only in the **Soviet Union**, but also in other Eastern European countries.

SEE ALSO Cause

Continuity

In the course of human history many things change, but there are also things that do not change, that continue to stay the same for a long period of time. This is known as continuity. An example might be the years between the late 1940s and the 1990s. During this time there were many localised conflicts but the overall hostility between the **Soviet Union** and the USA continued.

SEE ALSO Change; Cold War

Crick, Francis

Francis Crick was a Cambridge scientist who, with James Watson, worked out the double helix structure of deoxyribonucleic acid, DNA. This is the material of genes via which hereditary characteristics are passed on from parent to child. In 1962 Crick and Watson were awarded the Nobel Prize for Medicine.

SEE ALSO Watson, James

Cuban Missile Crisis

In October 1962 the United States gained proof from aerial photographs that the **Soviet Union** had placed nuclear missiles in Cuba. These put every major US city within range of a missile attack. The US President **John F. Kennedy** told the Soviet leader **Nikita Khrushchev** to withdraw the missiles. The US navy blockaded Cuba to prevent the arrival of any more Soviet ships carrying missiles. For thirteen days the world was on the brink of a nuclear war until the two leaders reached a compromise. Soviet missiles would be withdrawn from Cuba and US missiles would be withdrawn from Turkey.

One short-term consequence of this was the setting up of a hotline between the two leaders to try to avoid any future confrontations.

A longer-term consequence was that Khrushchev lost face and this led eventually to his fall from power.

Historians' interpretations of this crisis vary. Below are two very different views.

Kennedy the hero

When the crisis ended many people admired Kennedy for standing up to the aggression of Khrushchev. Kennedy received widespread support for insisting that the Soviet missiles had to be dismantled and taken away. Recent historians have also praised Kennedy's restraint. Despite heavy pressure from his own generals he refused to allow a US air strike against the missiles or an invasion of Cuba. These historians argue that that would have led to a full-scale exchange of nuclear weapons – nuclear war.

Kennedy the villain
After the crisis ended some people believed that it was Kennedy's fault because he had presented such a weak and inexperienced image to the Soviet Union. Some historians have gone further and accused him of over-reacting when the missiles were first discovered. They argue that Kennedy was keen to present a view of himself as a strong president dealing toughly with the Soviets. They argue that he did this in order to gain domestic support for his party in the US elections that were due to be held in November. So in their view he risked nuclear war just to increase his own personal popularity.

SEE ALSO Cold War; Interpretation

Curie, Marie

The scientist who, with her husband Pierre, discovered the element radium. Marie Curie won two Nobel Prizes for her work, in 1903 and in 1911.

D-Day

On 6 June 1944 British, Canadian and US troops landed on five beaches on the Normandy coast of France. This was the start of the liberation of France (and later Belgium and the Netherlands) from German occupation in the **Second World War**.

De Gaulle, Charles

Charles de Gaulle was the French general who led the Free French troops who fought on after France surrendered to Germany in the **Second World War**. After the war he went on to become president of France. As president he opposed Britain's application to become a member of the **Common Market**.

SEE ALSO Vichy France

Depression

Following the **Wall Street Crash** in October 1929 there was a collapse in economic activity around the world. This led to high unemployment and poverty in many countries. In some countries, such as Germany and Italy, people turned to extreme political parties to try to put things right. The increase in arms production in many countries in the lead-up to the **Second World War** was one reason why the Depression came to an end. It is sometimes called the Great Depression.

Détente

Détente is the word used to describe the easing of tension between the USA and the **Soviet Union** at the end of the **Cold War** in the 1980s. There were a number of features of this:

- The Vietnam War had ended.
- The USA and China were enjoying more friendly relations.
- People in all countries were worried about the nuclear arms race, both because of the threat of nuclear war and because of its cost.
- US astronauts and Soviet cosmonauts met and shook hands in space.
- The US and Soviet leaders held summit meetings such as **SALT I**.

Domino theory

This theory compared the countries in South East Asia to a row of dominoes. Once one domino fell over (or became **communist**) it would knock over the next one and so on. This led the USA to try to stop **Vietnam** from being taken over by the communists under Ho Chi Minh.

SEE ALSO Cold War

Dunkirk

In May 1940 at the start of the **Second World War**, British troops crossed to France to fight against the advancing Germans, just as they had done in the **First World War**. This time the German attack was so fast and effective that the British had to retreat to the Channel coast. To save them from capture the British organised Operation Dynamo. This involved not just the British navy but also over 800 small boats taken by their owners to help evacuate the troops. In the end, 338,000 soldiers were evacuated but 68,000 were lost.

The **propaganda** produced by the British government portrayed this as a great moment in history, but in reality it was a great defeat. As well as the loss of men, the British army left behind 120,000 vehicles, 90,000 rifles and 2300 guns.

SEE ALSO Blitzkrieg

Einstein, Albert

Albert Einstein was a German-born physicist. He is most famous for his revolutionary theory of the nature of space and time, known as the General Theory of Relativity.

European Union

The European Union was founded in 1958 by six countries. It was then called the Common Market. Denmark, Ireland and Britain became full members in 1973, Greece joined in 1981, Portugal and Spain in 1986, and Austria, Finland and Sweden in 1995. Its current name, the European Union, dates from the Treaty of Maastricht in 1992. In February 2007, there were 27 members. The single European currency, the euro, was officially adopted in 1999 by 13 member states.

SEE ALSO Common Market

Evidence

Evidence is what historians use to support their ideas about the past. They take this evidence from the historical **sources** that they study.

Fascism

This political idea has a number of characteristics. It is in favour of the following:
- **nationalism**
- a powerful leader or dictator
- one-party government
- national unity
- paramilitary organisations
- war.

SEE ALSO Hitler, Adolf; Mussolini, Benito

First World War

The war was triggered by the **assassination at Sarajevo** of Franz Ferdinand, heir to the throne of the Austro-Hungarian Empire. Its long-term causes were:
- the system of secret alliances, the **Triple Alliance** and the **Triple Entente**, which ensured that other European countries were pulled into a local conflict between Austria and Serbia
- **colonialism** – the rivalry between the European countries in building up their overseas empires which led to suspicion and hostility between, for example, Britain and Germany
- **nationalism** – the traditional empires such as Austria–Hungary were threatened by the desire of people such as the Slavs to have their own country
- naval rivalry between Germany and Britain
- militarism – in many European countries large armed forces were built up and this encouraged their leaders to consider using force.

Look at the world map on the next page which shows the countries involved in this war and the main theatres of fighting.

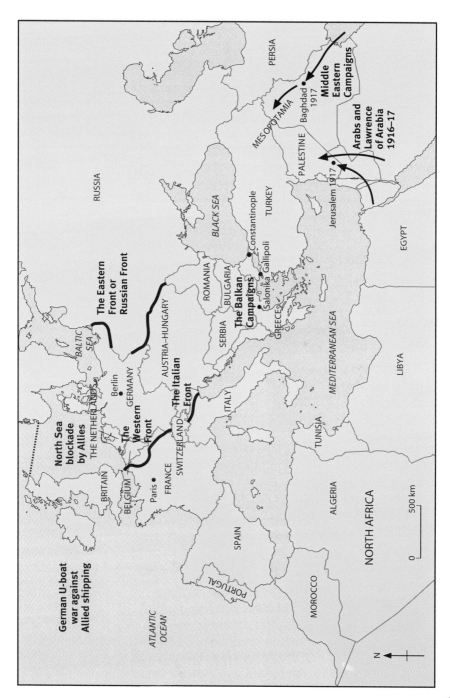

German U-boat
war against
Allied shipping

North Sea
blockade
by Allies

The Eastern
Front or
Russian Front

The
Western
Front

The Italian
Front

The Balkan
Campaigns

Middle
Eastern
Campaigns

Arabs and
Lawrence
of Arabia
1916–17

PERSIA

MESOPOTAMIA

Baghdad
1917

PALESTINE

Jerusalem 1917

EGYPT

RUSSIA

BLACK SEA

TURKEY

Constantinople

Gallipoli

Salonika

BULGARIA

ROMANIA

GREECE

SERBIA

AUSTRIA–HUNGARY

BALTIC
SEA

Berlin

GERMANY

THE NETHERLANDS

SWITZERLAND

ITALY

MEDITERRANEAN SEA

LIBYA

TUNISIA

BRITAIN

BELGIUM

Paris

FRANCE

SPAIN

PORTUGAL

MOROCCO

ALGERIA

NORTH AFRICA

ATLANTIC
OCEAN

N

0   500 km

Continued overleaf

This conflict lasted from 1914 to 1918 and the Allies were the eventual winners. However, by its end more than 8.5 million people had died and 21 million people were wounded.

SEE ALSO Gallipoli; Haig, General Sir Douglas; Schlieffen Plan; Somme; Trench warfare; Versailles, Treaty of; War poetry; Western Front; Ypres

Ford, Henry

Henry Ford was the founder of the motor company of that name. He is the man credited with the development of mass production which is so important for all industries today. His slogan to sell his Ford Model 'T' cars was, 'You can have any colour you want as long as it's black'. He was also famously quoted as saying, 'History is bunk'.

Gallipoli

In April 1915 the British launched an attack on Turkey at Gallipoli. The attack was the idea of **Winston Churchill** and it was designed to knock Turkey out of the **First World War**. However, the campaign was a complete failure. The troops had been given very little training in fighting on beaches and the Turkish troops were ready. The result was heavy losses of British, Australian and New Zealand troops. By January 1916, the Allied troops were evacuated by the navy.

Gandhi, Mohandas

An influential campaigner for India's independence from the **British Empire**, Gandhi used non-violent methods of passive resistance which were very successful. He was imprisoned on a number of occasions, but in August 1947 India achieved independence. Unfortunately, Gandhi did not live to enjoy this for long, as he was assassinated in January 1948. His influence continued as he inspired others such as the civil rights protesters in the USA.

SEE ALSO King, Martin Luther

Glasnost

In 1985 Mikhail Gorbachev became leader of the **Soviet Union**. He believed that the communist system needed to change in order to survive. He encouraged people to question the Government openly in order to improve it. This openness was known as *Glasnost*.

However, the Soviet people, not content with just criticising **communism**, wanted to get rid of it altogether. So, too, did the peoples of Eastern Europe. Gorbachev had fallen from power by 1992, and communism ended in Bulgaria, Czechoslovakia, East Germany, Hungary, Poland and Romania.

SEE ALSO Iron Curtain; Warsaw Pact

Haig, General Sir Douglas

A British commander in the **First World War**, Haig has been called the Butcher of the Somme by those who blame his tactics for the huge loss of life during that battle. The ordinary British soldiers who died are sometimes described as 'lions led by donkeys'. Haig was later promoted to field marshal and rewarded with honours after the war.

SEE ALSO Attrition; Somme

Hitler, Adolf

Adolf Hitler was the leader of Germany from 1933 to 1945. He was born in Austria in 1889. His early ambition was to become a painter but he was unsuccessful, and by 1914 he was living in poverty in Vienna. He fought in the German army in the **First World War**, winning the Iron Cross for bravery.

After the war he became leader of the German Nazi Party, which advocated **fascist** ideas. In 1923 he led the Munich Putsch, an unsuccessful attempt to overthrow the **Weimar Republic**. Hitler was then sent to prison, where he wrote his famous book, *Mein Kampf* (*My Struggle*), in which he put forward his ideas. Released from prison he continued to lead the Nazi Party, which gained increasing support from the German electorate. From 1933 onwards he was leader (*Führer*) of Germany.

Hitler's aggressive foreign policy is regarded as the major cause of the **Second World War**. At the end of the war he committed suicide to avoid capture by the advancing Soviet armies.

SEE ALSO Holocaust

Holocaust

In 1939 there were 8 million Jews living in Europe. Between 1939 and 1945, 6 million Jewish men, women and children were murdered in the parts of Europe controlled by the Nazis. This attempt to wipe out the Jewish population by the Nazis is usually known as the Holocaust. The Nazis called it the Final Solution. To begin with, Jews were either shot or confined in areas of cities set aside for them, known as ghettos. However, as the Nazis conquered Eastern Europe, more and more Jews came under their control. The Nazis now enlarged some of their existing concentration camps and set up death or extermination camps, such as Auschwitz and Treblinka, in remote areas of Eastern Europe. The Jews were sent in cattle trucks on the railways to these camps, where they were either worked to death, gassed or shot. This genocide was largely kept secret from the German people and from Germany's enemies, although there were rumours about what was happening in the camps.

There was resistance from some Jews. Jewish resistance fighters were active in German-occupied countries, and there were battles in the ghettos and sometimes in the camps themselves. For example, the death camp at Treblinka was set on fire in 1943.

Some people don't like the use of the term 'Holocaust', which means 'sacrifice', and instead prefer to use the term 'Churban', which means 'destruction'.

SEE ALSO Hitler, Adolf

Home Front

In the two World Wars this was the phrase used to describe what happened at home in Britain. In both wars industry changed to produce war materials, people had to put up with rationing and shortages of certain items normally imported from abroad and, particularly in the **Second World War**, people had to endure heavy bombing of the cities.

SEE ALSO Zeppelins

Imperialism

This can be defined as a policy of extending a country's influence in one of three ways. The first is through **colonialism**, as in, for example, the **British Empire.** The second is through military force, as in the case of Nazi Germany at the start of the **Second World War**. The third is through the use of economic power, a policy some would argue the USA carries out today.

Interpretation

An interpretation of history is a conscious attempt to portray the past in a certain way. It is a version of the past. It might be a historian trying to give a balanced view about a period, person or event. It might equally be someone deliberately attempting to portray the past in a certain way to further their own ends, such as an advertiser trying to sell something, a politician trying to prove a point, or a film or television programme maker trying to entertain. Just like **sources**, interpretations are useful to us as historians, and we need to be careful in deciding how far we can rely on them before we use them.

The television comedy series set in the **First World War**, *Blackadder Goes Forth*, is a good example, with its stereotypical view of generals as bumbling fools living lives of luxury far behind the front line. In one memorable quote Captain Blackadder describes the next attack as an attempt 'to move General **Haig's** drinks cabinet six inches closer to Berlin'. This stereotype can be challenged by the statistic that 78 British generals were killed in action or died on active service during the First World War.

Iron Curtain

In his famous speech at Fulton, Missouri, USA in 1946, **Winston Churchill** said, 'From Stettin in the Baltic to Trieste in the Adriatic an iron curtain has descended across the continent'. He was referring to the division between the West and all those countries of Eastern Europe that came under Soviet control at the end of the **Second World War** after they had been freed from Nazi occupation by Soviet troops. No sooner had the Allies defeated Germany than the differences between them came to the surface and the **Cold War** began.

SEE ALSO Soviet Union

Jutland

Despite the strong navies that Britain and Germany had built up before the **First World War**, neither side was anxious to fight a major battle at sea, as so much was at stake. In May 1916 the two fleets finally met at the Battle of Jutland. Britain lost more ships and men but the German fleet returned to port, giving Britain control of the seas for the rest of the war.

Kennedy, John F.

Charismatic president of the USA from 1961 until his assassination in 1963, Kennedy was born in 1917 into a rich and powerful family. In the **Second World War** he commanded a torpedo boat in the Pacific War against Japan. After one fight he was wounded and also decorated for bravery. When the war ended he went into politics, representing the Democratic party. As president, after the **Cuban Missile Crisis** he was instrumental in the setting up of a 'hotline' between himself and the Soviet leader **Nikita Khrushchev**. Its purpose was to enable the two leaders to talk and thus avoid any danger of a similar crisis leading to nuclear war.

Khrushchev, Nikita

Leader of the **Soviet Union** between 1955 and 1964, Khrushchev was the son of a coal-miner. He fought in the Red Army during the civil war which followed the **Russian Revolution**. He played an important role in the defence of **Stalingrad** during the **Second World War**. He then rose through the ranks of the Communist Party and, following the death of **Stalin**, was able to come to power. He relaxed some of the more repressive measures of Stalin's rule but came into conflict with the USA on a number of occasions, the most serious being the **Cuban Missile Crisis** which almost led to a nuclear war. He was forced to retire in 1964 and died in 1971.

King, Martin Luther

Martin Luther King was a US black civil rights leader who argued in favour of using non-violent methods to achieve equality for all races in the USA. In his famous speech in 1963 he said,
'I have a dream that one day this nation will rise up and live out the true meaning of its creed: We hold these truths to be self-evident, that all men are created equal. I have a dream that the sons of former slaves and the sons of former slave owners would sit down together at the table of brotherhood.'
He was assassinated in April 1968.

SEE ALSO Gandhi, Mohandas

Korean War

See the maps on the next two pages.
At the end of the **Second World War** the country of Korea was freed from Japanese occupation by the **Soviet Union** in the north and by the USA in the south. The country was divided in two on the line of the 38th parallel (line of latitude). The Soviets set up a Communist government in North Korea under Kim Il Sung while the USA set up elections which led to Syngman Rhee leading South Korea. Both the Soviet Union and the USA withdrew their troops.
On 25 June 1950, with the backing of **Stalin**, North Korea invaded the south. South Korea was only saved by the arrival of **United Nations** troops sent by several countries including the USA and Britain. These troops drove the North Koreans back and it was then only the intervention of **Mao Zedong's** China that saved North Korea from being overrun. The two sides ended up facing each other roughly along the line of the 38th parallel. **Armistice** talks began in 1951 and dragged on until 1953 when a truce was arranged.
One feature of the war in the air was that the US air force was fighting Soviet planes with Chinese markings flown by Soviet pilots wearing Chinese uniforms. Both sides kept this secret.
The death toll was heavy. The UN forces lost 94,000 troops, the North Koreans and Chinese together lost 1.5 million and about a million civilian Koreans also died.

SEE ALSO Cold War

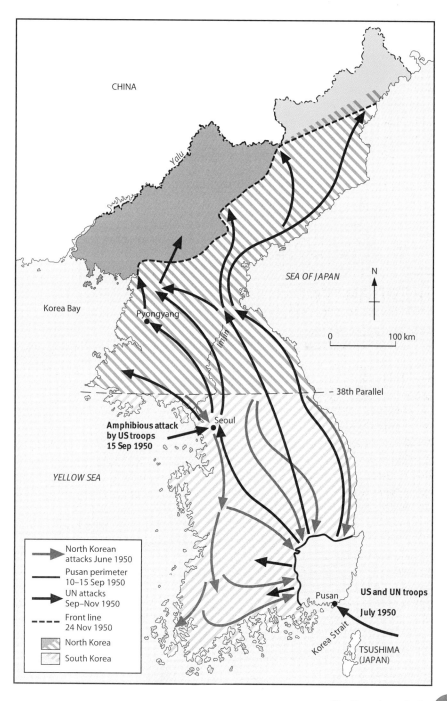

CHINA

Yalu

Korea Bay

SEA OF JAPAN

N

Pyongyang

Imjin

0   100 km

38th Parallel

Amphibious attack
by US troops
15 Sep 1950

Seoul

YELLOW SEA

North Korean
attacks June 1950

Pusan perimeter
10–15 Sep 1950

UN attacks
Sep–Nov 1950

Front line
24 Nov 1950

North Korea

South Korea

Pusan

US and UN troops

July 1950

Korea Strait

TSUSHIMA
(JAPAN)

Continued overleaf

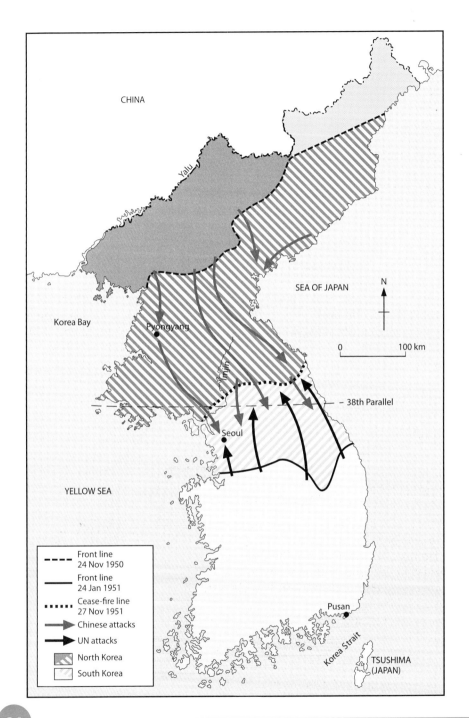

CHINA

Yalu

Korea Bay

Pyongyang

SEA OF JAPAN

N

0   100 km

Imjin

38th Parallel

Seoul

YELLOW SEA

Pusan

Korea Strait

TSUSHIMA
(JAPAN)

Front line
24 Nov 1950

Front line
24 Jan 1951

Cease-fire line
27 Nov 1951

Chinese attacks

UN attacks

North Korea

South Korea

League of Nations

The League of Nations was set up in 1918 due to the influence of the US President **Woodrow Wilson**. Its main purpose was to settle disputes between countries peacefully so that there would not be another destructive war like the **First World War**. While it was successful in solving some problems in the 1920s, it was basically too weak to act when major countries attacked weaker countries, such as when Japan attacked China in 1931 or when Italy invaded Abyssinia in 1935.
Its main weaknesses were that:
- Germany was not allowed to join at first
- the USA did not join – Congress did not agree with the President
- it had no army to back it up.

Lenin, Vladimir Ilyich

Lenin was the leader of the **Soviet Union** from 1917 to 1924. He was born in 1870 into a respectable family. His older brother was hanged for plotting against the Tsar. Lenin was a revolutionary, influenced by the ideas of **Karl Marx**. As a revolutionary he spent part of his life in prison and part living in exile. When the Tsar's government collapsed in 1917 Lenin returned to Russia. He led the successful Bolshevik Revolution in 1917 and became the first leader of the Soviet Union. After his death in 1924 **Stalin** became the next leader.

SEE ALSO Russian Revolution

Mao Zedong

Mao Zedong was the leader of China from 1949 to 1976. He was born in 1893, the son of a peasant farmer. He became the leader of the Chinese **communist** forces who in 1949 won the civil war that followed the end of the **Second World War**. In 1950 he sent Chinese troops to help the North Koreans. In 1958 he launched 'The Great Leap Forward' which was designed to develop China's industry, but very poor harvests led to its failure. In 1966 he launched the Cultural Revolution to bring China back to communist principles, using the student Red Guards to enforce his policies.

Continued overleaf

His sayings were collected in the 'Little Red Book'. He remained in power until his death in 1976. Some historians regard Mao as the biggest mass murderer of the twentieth century, responsible for the deaths of more millions of people than either **Hitler** or **Stalin**. In their biography of Mao, *Mao: The Unknown Story*, Jung Chang and Jon Halliday argue that he caused the deaths of over 70 million Chinese.

SEE ALSO Korean War

Marx, Karl

Karl Marx was a political thinker whose ideas had a huge impact on the twentieth century. He wrote that in a **capitalist** country like Britain or the USA the owners of the means of production – the mills, mines, factories and workshops – had the power. But it was the workers (the 'proletariat') who actually produced the wealth. He argued that the workers would rise up against their capitalist owners in a violent revolution to set up a 'dictatorship of the proletariat'. The state would take over ownership of land, banks, factories and  businesses. Pure **communism** would be achieved when everyone worked for the good of all, and took back only enough for their needs.

SEE ALSO Lenin, Vladimir Ilyich; Russian Revolution

Mussolini, Benito

Mussolini became leader of Italy in 1922 with his **Fascist** Party. He followed an aggressive foreign policy and invaded Abyssinia in 1935 as part of his plan to build a second Roman Empire. The **League of Nations** failed to stop him, partly because Britain and France wanted him as an ally against Germany. Mussolini went on to form an alliance with **Hitler's** Nazi Germany in the **Second World War**. When Italy was defeated Mussolini fell from power. In April 1945 he was seized by his enemies, shot and then hung upside down for public display.

Nationalism

Nationalism means a sense of belonging to a nation. The people of a nation usually have some of the following in common:
- language
- culture
- religion
- tradition/history
- ethnicity.

Of course, some nations that you can think of do not entirely fit this definition. What is important is that the people feel they are a nation. In the twentieth century nationalism has been both a force for good and a force for evil.

SEE ALSO Fascism

NATO

In 1949 relations between the two sides in the **Cold War** were getting worse after the **Berlin Blockade or Airlift**. So in that year the USA, Britain, Canada, France and Italy set up the North Atlantic Treaty Organisation (NATO). West Germany joined in 1955. This was a military alliance aimed at defending its members against the **Soviet Union**. After the collapse of the Soviet Union and the **Warsaw Pact**, NATO has continued to exist as a way for its members to work together, for example, by leading a peacekeeping force in Kosovo since 1992.

Olympic boycott

In 1980 the USA withdrew its athletes from the Olympic Games, which were being held in Moscow, as a protest against the Soviet invasion of **Afghanistan**. In 1984 the **Soviet Union** retaliated by withdrawing its athletes from the Olympic Games which were being held in Los Angeles. This is a good example of how both sides in the **Cold War** used sport to compete against each other.

Oppenheimer, Robert

Robert Oppenheimer was the scientist who led the team that carried out the basic research for the **atomic bomb**, then designed and built it. This was part of the secret 'Manhattan Project', which was based in the USA during the **Second World War**. The project led to the development and growth of the new city of Los Alamos in the desert in New Mexico in the USA.

Pearl Harbor

On 7 December 1941 the Japanese made a surprise attack on the US naval base at Pearl Harbor in Hawaii. In two hours eighteen US warships were sunk or wrecked, 177 US planes were destroyed, most of them still on the ground, and 2300 Americans were killed. The Japanese lost 29 planes. This attack brought the USA into the **Second World War** against Japan and also Germany.

Pétain, Henri

During the **First World War**, Henri Pétain was the French commander at **Verdun** and was later promoted to the rank of Marshal of France. In the **Second World War** he became the leader of **Vichy France**, which collaborated with Nazi Germany. When the war ended he was arrested, tried and convicted for treason. He was sentenced to death but this was changed to life imprisonment.

Potsdam Conference

In July 1945 the **Second World War** was over in Europe. The three main Allied leaders – **Winston Churchill, Josef Stalin** and Harry S. Truman – met at Potsdam, a suburb of Berlin. At the Yalta Conference earlier that year they had reached agreement on most issues but by the time they met at Potsdam, a number of things had changed:

- The USA had a new president. **Roosevelt** died in April 1945 and was replaced by Truman, who was much more anti-**communist**.
- Stalin's armies were occupying most of Eastern Europe and refugees were fleeing these countries, fearing a communist takeover.
- Stalin had set up a Communist government in Poland, against the wishes of the majority of Poles.
- The Allies had successfully tested an **atomic bomb**.

The leaders were unable to agree on what to do with Germany. Stalin wanted to leave Germany crippled and also wanted reparations (compensation payments for the war). But the Allies wanted to avoid repeating the mistakes they had made at **Versailles** at the end of the **First World War**, when Germany had received harsh penalties. This had led to resentment among the German people, which was one of the causes of the Second World War. The meeting ended without agreement and the **Cold War** developed.

Propaganda

Information which is spread by a government to influence people's opinions is called propaganda. It may show events in a better light than they actually were, such as when a government tries to give the impression that a military defeat was a victory, or it may even be blatantly untrue.

SEE ALSO Cold War, Dunkirk

Reliability

All historians are careful to check on **source** reliability, that is, how far they can rely on or trust what they learn from each of their sources, including any figures quoted. They do this by asking these questions:
- Who produced it? Who were they working for? Were they likely to be telling the truth?
- Why was it produced? (In other words, what was its purpose?) Was it produced to give a fair and accurate account of the past? Was it produced to influence a particular person or group of people? Are any figures quoted accurate?
- Who was it produced for? What was its intended audience?
- When and where was it produced?

The answers to these questions help historians to decide how far they can rely upon each source before they begin to use it.

SEE ALSO Utility

Reunification of Germany

The decline of the **Soviet Union** and the end of the **Cold War** allowed for German reunification. The two halves of the country, divided at the end of the **Second World War**, were reunited on 3 October 1990 after the collapse of the **Communist** government of East Germany. This brought together one of the most affluent **capitalist** countries with one of the most prosperous socialist countries from the Eastern bloc.

Roosevelt, Franklin Delano

Roosevelt was president of the USA from 1933 to 1945. He was born in 1882 into a rich New York family. After training as a lawyer he went into politics. In 1921 he was paralysed by polio and spent the rest of his life in a wheelchair. He became president in 1933 at the height of the **Depression**. His policies to help the unemployed and to restart the economy, known as the New Deal, made him very popular. He was elected president four times and led the USA in the **Second World War**. He died before it ended, in April 1945.

Russian Revolution

In 1917 Tsar Nicholas II of Russia was overthrown by a revolution when his own soldiers joined the protesting workers instead of fighting them. The workers were protesting against the hardships of their lives. As a result of Russia's involvement in the **First World War** there were food shortages. Some industries closed down due to a lack of fuel, which led to unemployment, while those still in work were being asked to work longer hours. At the same time Russian casualties in the fighting were rising and people lost confidence in the government.

In October 1917 the Bolsheviks, led by **Lenin**, took over leadership of this revolution. The Bolsheviks went on to win the civil war that followed and set up the **communist** state of the **Soviet Union**. The Tsar and his family were killed, along with several million of their former subjects.

Rutherford, Ernest

Ernest Rutherford was a New Zealand-born scientist. From 1919, he supervised the experiments at Cambridge which led, in 1932, to the splitting of the atom. This was a major breakthrough which made possible the later development of the **atomic bomb**.

SALT I and SALT II

The Strategic Arms Limitation Talks (SALT) were talks between the leaders of the USA and the **Soviet Union**. They reflected the anxiety of people around the world about the threat of nuclear war as a result of the **Cold War**. Both sides possessed enough weapons to wipe out the world.

In 1972 at SALT I, US President Richard Nixon and Soviet President Leonid Brezhnev agreed to limit the number of ICBMs (intercontinental ballistic missiles) that they built.

In 1979 at SALT II, US President Jimmy Carter and Soviet President Leonid Brezhnev agreed more cuts in ICBMs, although this agreement was scrapped after a disagreement over the Soviet invasion of **Afghanistan**.

Schlieffen Plan

This was the plan devised by German generals in the **First World War** to cope with having to fight a war on two fronts, against France in the west and Russia in the east. The German armies would bypass the French frontier defences by attacking through Belgium, encircling Paris and forcing the French to surrender. Then their armies could turn east to fight the Russians, who were expected to take much longer to mobilise their armies. See the map on the next page.

In practice the plan failed because:

- the small Belgian army provided unexpectedly strong resistance, as did the British troops sent to help
- the German troops were exhausted by advancing so far so quickly and were not able to encircle Paris
- the French were able to move troops north to meet and fight the Germans
- Russia mobilised much more quickly than expected and some German armies had to be moved to the Eastern Front to halt their invasion.

The German advance was halted and the conflict continued as static **trench warfare**.

SEE ALSO Western Front

Continued overleaf

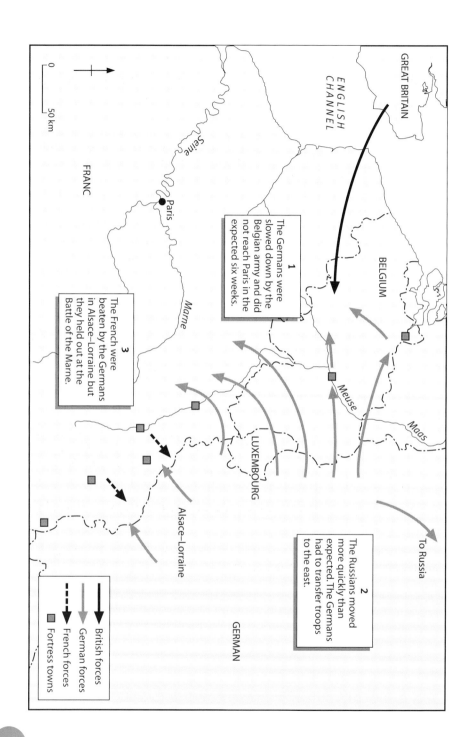

GREAT BRITAIN

ENGLISH CHANNEL

BELGIUM

FRANC

Paris

Seine

Marne

Meuse

Maas

LUXEMBOURG

Alsace–Lorraine

GERMAN

0
50 km

1
The Germans were slowed down by the Belgian army and did not reach Paris in the expected six weeks.

3
The French were beaten by the Germans in Alsace–Lorraine but they held out at the Battle of the Marne.

2
The Russians moved more quickly than expected. The Germans had to transfer troops to the east.

To Russia

British forces
German forces
French forces
Fortress towns

Second World War

The Second World War lasted from 1939 to 1945. Its causes can be grouped under four major headings:

Hitler's plans
Adolf Hitler, leader of Germany, wanted to abolish the **Treaty of Versailles**, expand German territory and defeat **communism**. As a result he rearmed Germany and followed an aggressive foreign policy.

The policy of appeasement
This policy meant trying to keep the peace rather than challenging Germany. Britain and France were anxious to avoid another war after the losses of the **First World War**. Many people in these countries agreed that the Treaty of Versailles was unfair in some ways. They were also more afraid of communism than they were of Hitler.

The Nazi-Soviet Pact
Fearing that Britain and France were willing to let Hitler attack Eastern Europe, including the **Soviet Union, Stalin** decided to enter into an agreement with Hitler, a pact which they signed in 1939. They agreed to split Poland between them.

The failures of the League of Nations
While the League was successful in solving some problems in the 1920s, it was too weak to act when major countries attacked weaker countries. It was therefore unable to stop the aggression of either Hitler's Germany or Stalin's Soviet Union.

See the next page for a world map which shows where the fighting took place between the two sides.

This was an immensely destructive conflict. The figures on page 35, which are approximate, show the scale of the military and civilian casualties.

Continued overleaf

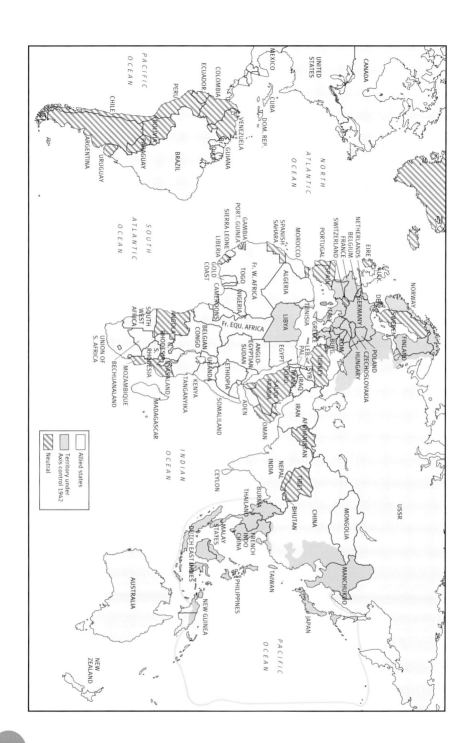

PACIFIC OCEAN

MEXICO
UNITED STATES
CANADA

COLOMBIA
ECUADOR
PERU
CHILE
VENEZUELA
GUIANA
BRAZIL
BOLIVIA
PARAGUAY
URUGUAY
ARGENTINA

CUBA
DOM. REP.

NORTH ATLANTIC OCEAN

SOUTH ATLANTIC OCEAN

GREENLAND

NORWAY
SWEDEN
FINLAND
DENMARK
U.K.
EIRE
NETHERLANDS
BELGIUM
SWITZERLAND
FRANCE
PORTUGAL
SPAIN
GERMANY
POLAND
CZECHOSLOVAKIA
HUNGARY
ROM.
BULG.
GREECE
ITALY
TURKEY

MOROCCO
SPANISH SAHARA
ALGERIA
TUNISIA
LIBYA
EGYPT
GAMBIA
PORT. GUINEA
SIERRA LEONE
LIBERIA
GOLD COAST
TOGO
Fr. W. AFRICA
NIGERIA
CAMEROONS
Fr. EQU. AFRICA
ANGLO-EGYPTIAN SUDAN
BELGIAN CONGO
UGANDA
ETHIOPIA
SOMALILAND
KENYA
TANGANYIKA
ANGOLA
RHODESIA
S. RHODESIA
NYASALAND
SOUTH WEST AFRICA
BECHUANALAND
MOZAMBIQUE
MADAGASCAR
UNION OF S. AFRICA

LEB.
SYRIA
PAL.
TRANS JORD.
IRAQ
SAUDI ARABIA
OMAN
ADEN
IRAN
AFGHANISTAN

INDIAN OCEAN

USSR

NEPAL
TIBET
INDIA
CEYLON
BHUTAN
BURMA
THAILAND
FRENCH INDO CHINA
MALAY STATES
DUTCH EAST INDIES
PHILIPPINES
TAIWAN
CHINA
MONGOLIA
MANCHUKUO
JAPAN

AUSTRALIA
NEW GUINEA
NEW ZEALAND

PACIFIC OCEAN

Allied states
Territory under
Axis control 1942
Neutral

Casualties of the Second World War

	Military millions	Civilian millions	Total millions
Britain	0.33	0.06	0.39
France	0.34	0.47	0.81
USA	0.30	–	0.30
Soviet Union	8.70	16.90	25.60
Poland	0.85	6.00	6.85
Yugoslavia	0.30	1.40	1.70
China	1.30	10.00	11.30
Germany	3.30	3.80	7.10
Italy	0.33	0.08	0.41
Japan	1.50	0.30	1.80

SEE ALSO Atomic bomb; Blitzkrieg; Dunkirk; Potsdam Conference; Stalingrad; Yalta Conference

Significance

With so much to study historians have to make decisions on the significance of individuals and events. This is an important skill. This book contains details of many individuals, such as Ernest Rutherford, whose significance is clear because of how their lives affected the lives of many others at the time they lived and later. Who do you think is most significant?

Somme

On 1 July 1916 the British army under General **Haig** launched a major attack on the German trenches along the River Somme in France. After a seven-day bombardment designed to destroy the German defenders, the British troops advanced across 'no man's land', only to find the German trenches well defended. There were around 57,000 British casualties on the first day, the heaviest loss ever sustained by a British army in a single day or by any army in the **First World War**.

SEE ALSO Attrition; Trench warfare; Western Front

Source

A source can be many different things: an artefact (object made by people), building, diary, letter, film, map, newspaper, painting, photograph, object, report – to name just a few. A source is anything from which historians can gather **evidence** to help them to find out about the past.

SEE ALSO Reliability; Utility

Soviet Union

The Soviet Union was the name usually given to the Union of Soviet Socialist Republics (USSR), which emerged as a country at the end of the civil war that followed the **Russian Revolution** of 1917. It took its name from the Soviets, the workers' councils that became part of the system of government at local, regional and national level. Following the execution (or some would say murder) of the Tsar and his family, the country became a republic. It is sometimes wrongly referred to as Russia during this period. In 1991 the **Communist** Party lost power and the Soviet Union broke up into a number of independent states, including Russia and smaller states such as Estonia and the Ukraine.

SEE ALSO Glasnost; Khrushchev, Nikita; Lenin, Vladimir Ilyich; Stalin, Josef

Stalin, Josef

Stalin was the leader of the **Soviet Union** from 1924 to 1953. He was born in 1879 in Georgia, the son of a shoemaker. His original name was Josef Djugashvili but like many revolutionaries he changed his name. 'Stalin' means 'man of steel' – which says something about his character. Stalin was a former Bolshevik and managed to take control of the Soviet Union after **Lenin's** death in 1924. He held power until his own death in 1953.
He was renowned for his ruthlessness. During the years 1932 to 1938, known as The Great Terror, his opponents were condemned after show trials and then executed or imprisoned in labour camps. The following saying is attributed to him, 'A single death is a tragedy but a million deaths are just a statistic'.

Stalingrad

In 1942 the German invasion of the **Soviet Union** had reached the city of Stalingrad. The fighting which followed was some of the fiercest of the **Second World War**. Both sides poured in troops in an effort to win. Eventually the German forces were surrounded and forced to surrender. From then on they were on the defensive in the Soviet Union.

Tanks

On 15 September 1916, General **Haig** decided to use a new weapon – tanks. This first tank attack was not a great success. There were too few tanks available, some broke down and those that successfully penetrated the German trenches were not supported by infantry. However, the lesson of their potential was not lost on the Germans.

SEE ALSO Blitzkrieg; First World War; Trench warfare

Trench warfare

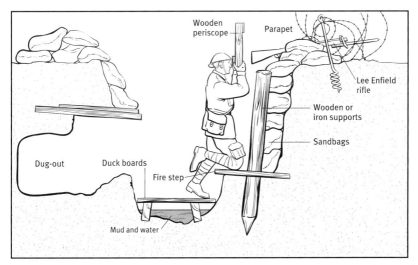

On the **Western Front** during the **First World War**, both sides built trenches as defensive positions with 'no man's land' separating the two lines of trenches. Since front-line duty was so stressful, soldiers usually spent just four days in the

Continued overleaf

front-line trenches, four days in support, four days in reserve and then fourteen days resting behind the lines. Of course, this was the theory and sometimes the reality was very different.

Even in front-line trenches, soldiers on both sides could go for long periods without seeing an enemy soldier. Their lives were not pleasant. In addition to the danger, they faced a number of problems:

- Soldiers suffered from boredom because of the long hours of inactivity.
- With so many men living so close together, sanitation arrangements were poor, with a combination of sewage and rotting corpses. It was little wonder that the trenches were also infested with rats.
- Individual soldiers were infested with lice, or 'chats' as they called them.
- In summer the trenches were hot, dusty and smelly. In winter they were cold and the men suffered from frostbite. In wet weather they filled with water and the soldiers suffered from 'trench foot' through standing in water for hours at a time.

SEE ALSO War poetry

Triple Alliance and Triple Entente

Triple Alliance	Triple Entente
Austria–Hungary	Britain
Germany	France
Italy	Russia

These were the two main hostile alliances in Europe at the start of the twentieth century, the existence of which was one of the long-term causes of the **First World War**. The countries on each side agreed to support fellow members of their alliance if they were involved in war.

SEE ALSO Balance of power

Truman Doctrine

In 1947 the US President Harry S. Truman promised financial and military aid to any country threatened by **communism**. This became known as the Truman Doctrine. It formed part of the US anti-communism foreign policy. This policy was also known as Containment.

SEE ALSO Cold War; Korean War

U-boats

In the **First World War** Germany built large numbers of *Unterseebooten* (U-boats or submarines) and used them to sink merchant ships bringing supplies to Britain. They were very effective until the British decided that ships should sail in large groups (convoys) protected by warships. One **consequence** of the U-boat campaign was that it brought the USA into the war after a U-boat sank the liner *Lusitania*. Among the 1000 people who drowned were 124 Americans.
In the **Second World War** the Germans once again used U-boats to attack British shipping with considerable success to start with. However, in the later stages of the war the U-boats were defeated by the combination of convoys and escort ships, together with long-range aircraft which were able to spot and attack the U-boats.

United Nations

In 1945 representatives of 50 countries met in San Francisco to set up the United Nations (UN). This was designed to replace the **League of Nations** and had the same aim of helping countries to resolve their differences peacefully. It was not allowed to interfere in the internal affairs of any of its member countries. It is now based in New York and has over 190 member countries.
Since it was set up the UN has been involved in many disputes around the world. Sometimes its troops have been sent to fight under the UN flag, such as in Korea in 1950. At other times its troops have been used to try to maintain peace by keeping the two sides apart, such as in the former country of Yugoslavia in 1992.

SEE ALSO Korean War

Utility

'How useful for my enquiry is this source?' is one of the most important questions that historians ask. In order to find out about the past they need to look at historical **sources**. They test all their sources by asking what they can learn from each source about the question that they are studying. They then go on to check how far they can rely on what the source is telling them by asking a further set of questions to test its **reliability**. 'Utility' is a measure of how useful a source really is.

Verdun

In February 1916 the Germans launched a major attack on the French trenches around Verdun in France. The German commander said that his aim was to 'bleed the French white'. The French were equally determined to hold Verdun, which was a symbol of national pride. By the time the battle ended in December the Germans had lost approximately 434,000 men while the French lost approximately 542,000. To the French this was a victory, despite the fact that their army was on the brink of mutiny. It made the reputation of their commander, Marshal **Pétain**.

SEE ALSO Attrition; First World War; Somme; Trench warfare; Western Front

Versailles, Treaty of

The peace treaty that ended the **First World War** was signed on 28 June 1919 at Versailles, France. The major decisions were made by the leaders of the three main Allied countries: David Lloyd George of Britain, Georges Clemenceau of France and **Woodrow Wilson** of the USA. The Germans were very unhappy with the terms but had to sign.
The terms of the treaty:
- Germany lost all the land it had gained.
- Germany lost all its colonies.
- Germany was forbidden from uniting with Austria.
- The German armed forces were severely limited.
- Germany had to sign the war guilt clause accepting blame for starting the war.
- Germany had to pay £6.6 million reparations (compensation) to the Allies to cover their costs.

With the benefit of hindsight, historians view this as the beginning of the chain of events that led eventually to the outbreak of the **Second World War**.

Vichy France

This was the part of France that was originally not occupied by the Germans after the French surrendered in 1940. For four years under the leadership of Marshal **Pétain** this part of France was governed from the town of Vichy and co-operated with the Germans. This left French people with a difficult decision to take – should they remain loyal to Vichy France, or join the Free French led by **Charles de Gaulle** or the Resistance to continue to fight Germany?

SEE ALSO Second World War

Vietnam War

In 1954 the French withdrew from their former colony of Vietnam which was under attack by the **communist** state of North Vietnam, led by Ho Chi Minh. The Americans were afraid that if South Vietnam fell to the communists then other countries would follow. The Americans became gradually more and more involved in the war until by 1965 over half a million of their troops were in South Vietnam. Despite their superior fire power it became obvious that the Americans could not win and the steady stream of deaths turned public opinion against the war. The Americans withdrew in 1973 and by 1975 the country was unified under the communists.

The Americans lost the war for a number of reasons:

- The Viet Cong were expert guerrilla fighters whose objective was to kill enemy soldiers and not to capture territory.
- The US soldiers were conscripts who only fought for one year and were therefore very inexperienced.
- The morale of the US forces was very low.
- The massive US bombing campaign which tried unsuccessfully to destroy the Viet Cong and the North Vietnamese army was very expensive.
- North Vietnam received military and economic aid from China and the **Soviet Union**.
- US public opinion turned against the war because of the loss of lives of US soldiers and because of the horrific images shown each evening on US television. The Vietnam War was in some ways a media war.

SEE ALSO Colonialism; Domino theory; Truman Doctrine

Wall Street Crash

In just one week in October 1929 the value of shares on the New York stock exchange located on Wall Street fell by 50 per cent. This was as a result of long-term factors:

- over-production in US industry
- a fall in demand for US goods at home and abroad
- the fact that roughly 50 per cent of Americans could only afford the bare necessities of life.

The crash was triggered by problems on the New York stock market. As so many people were keen to make money by buying shares their price went up well above their real value. When people realised this and started to sell their shares a panic set in, prices fell dramatically and people were financially ruined. This event is usually seen as the start of what is known as the **Depression**.

SEE ALSO Cause

War poetry

One of the most astonishingly beautiful things to emerge from the **First World War** on the **Western Front** was the writing of some young poets. Their poetry serves as a record of the views of some of those serving in the trenches on their situation and on their leaders. The two quoted below are both by Siegfried Sassoon, a lieutenant in the Royal Welsh Fusiliers. He was decorated for bravery and was wounded in the Battle of the **Somme**. In 1917 he made an official protest against the war, which he argued was unnecessary.

The General

'Good-morning: good-morning!' the General said
When we met him last week on the way to the line.
Now the soldiers he smiled at are most of 'em dead,
And we're cursing his staff for incompetent swine.
'He's a cheery old card,' grunted Harry to Jack
As they slogged up to Arras with rifle and pack.

But he did for them both by his plan of attack.

An extract from *Aftermath*

Do you remember the dark months you held the sector at Mametz –
The nights you watched and wired and dug and piled sandbags on parapets?
Do you remember the rats; and the stench
Of corpses rotting in the front of the front-line trench –
And dawn coming, dirty white, and chill with a hopeless rain?
Do you ever stop and ask, 'Is it all going to happen again?'

Do you remember that hour of din before the attack –
And the anger, the blind compassion that seized and shook you then
As you peered at the doomed and haggard faces of your men?
Do you remember the stretcher-cases lurching back
With dying eyes and lolling heads – those ashen-grey
Masks of the lads who once were keen and kind and gay?

Have you forgotten yet? …
Look up, and swear by the green of the spring that you'll never forget.

SEE ALSO Trench Warfare

Warsaw Pact

The Warsaw Pact was a military alliance linking the **Soviet Union** with the **communist** countries of Eastern Europe which included Bulgaria, Czechoslovakia, East Germany, Hungary, Poland and Romania. It was set up in 1955 as a direct response to the creation of **NATO**, which the communist countries saw as a threat to them. The pact lasted throughout the **Cold War** until 1991 when member countries began withdrawing after the collapse of communism in Eastern Europe and the Soviet Union.

Watson, James

James Watson was a Cambridge scientist who, with Francis Crick, worked out the double helix structure of deoxyribonucleic acid, DNA. This is the material of genes by which hereditary characteristics are passed on from parent to child. In 1962 Watson and Crick were awarded the Nobel Prize for Medicine.

SEE ALSO Crick, Francis

Weimar Republic

In 1919 the German ruler Kaiser Wilhelm II, who was blamed for defeat in the **First World War**, was forced to abdicate (resign). The new democratic German government was set up in the town of Weimar, hence its name – the Weimar Republic. Despite opposition from extremists on both sides, both the left-wing communists and the right-wing Nazis, the Weimar Republic survived until the effects of the **Depression** caused massive economic problems. This gave a boost to the extreme political parties and by 1933 the Nazis had gained control of Germany.

The Weimar Republic is often viewed as a failure but it is worth noting that it succeeded in running Germany for fourteen years through a time of great upheaval after the defeat in the First World War. What made things harder was that Germany was a country with no tradition of democratic government behind it.

SEE ALSO Fascism; Hitler, Adolf

Western Front

After the failure of the **Schlieffen Plan** at the outbreak of the **First World War**, the German armies began to dig trenches with machine gun posts on top to defend themselves. The British and French also built trenches. To make sure that the enemy could not outflank them, both sides extended their trenches so that eventually they stretched from the English Channel in the west to Switzerland in the east. This band of trenches, over 600 kilometres long, became known as the Western Front and was the scene of some of the heaviest fighting of the war.

SEE ALSO Attrition; Somme; Tanks; Trench warfare; Verdun; Ypres

Wilson, Woodrow

Woodrow Wilson was president of the USA during the **First World War**. He made a speech in January 1918 where he set out 'Fourteen Points' which he hoped would form the basis of the peace treaty after the war. These had some influence on the negotiations of the **Treaty of Versailles**. They included the following points:

- There should be no secret alliances between countries.
- There should be a reduction in arms.
- The people of Europe should be able to decide for themselves who they were ruled by (self-determination).

He also put forward the idea of the **League of Nations**, although he was unable to persuade the US Congress that the USA should join.

Yalta Conference

The Yalta Conference was held in February 1945, by which time it was clear that Germany was going to lose the **Second World War**. The three major Allied leaders – **Winston Churchill, Franklin D. Roosevelt** and **Josef Stalin** – met to decide how to treat Germany.

They agreed:
- to divide Germany into four zones – American, British, French and Soviet
- to hunt down and bring to justice those who had committed war crimes
- to allow each country that they freed from Nazi control to hold free elections to decide the government they wanted
- to join the new United Nations
- that Eastern Europe should be seen as a Soviet sphere of influence.

Their only area of disagreement was over Poland, some of which Stalin wanted to make part of the **Soviet Union**. However, things were very different when they met again at the **Potsdam Conference** in July and August 1945.

Ypres

The Germans, who for most of the **First World War** remained on the defensive on the **Western Front**, did attack on some occasions. At Ypres on 22 April 1915 they used poison gas for the first time. The plan was to kill the soldiers in the opposing trenches so that the German soldiers in their gas-proof helmets could safely cross 'no man's land' and capture them. The chlorine gas that they used burned men's lungs and blinded them.

Both sides used gas as a weapon during the war and their scientists developed more poison gases to use, such as mustard gas which burned, blinded or slowly killed its victims over four to five weeks. Both sides also developed very effective gas masks which their soldiers carried with them so that death from gas attacks became less of a real danger. Through the course of the whole war approximately 3000 British soldiers died from gassing.

Zeppelins

This was the name given to a type of rigid airship (hot air balloon) invented by Count Ferdinand von Zeppelin in 1900. In January 1915 German Zeppelins dropped bombs on Great Yarmouth and King's Lynn. This was the first of many bombing raids on British towns and cities carried out by these airships. The development of searchlights, anti-aircraft guns and fighter planes ended this threat by 1916 when bombing was carried out by bomber aircraft. About 1100 British people died as a result of all bombing raids in the **First World War**, so they were nothing like as destructive as the raids of the **Second World War**. After the war Zeppelins provided the first transatlantic airline service. This was stopped when the Zeppelin *Hindenburg* crashed and burned out in New York in May 1937 and people lost confidence in their safety.

SEE ALSO Home Front